SD
143
C 5.5

11/78

D1253928

THE GEO. S. LONG PUBLICATION SERIES

Man, Land,

and the Forest Environment

MARION CLAWSON

University of Washington Press

Seattle and London

Copyright © 1977 by the University of Washington Press
Printed in the United States of America

All rights reserved. No part of this publication may be reproduced or
transmitted in any form or by any means, electronic or mechanical,
including photocopy, recording, or any information storage or re-
trieval system, without permission in writing from the publisher.

Library of Congress Cataloging in Publication Data

Clawson, Marion, 1905–
    Man, land, and the forest environment.

    (The Geo. S. Long publication series)
    Bibliography: p.
    1.   Forests and forestry—United States—Addresses,
essays, lectures. 2.   Land use—Planning—United States
—Addresses, essays, lectures. 3.   Forest management—
United States—Addresses, essays, lectures. 4.   Forest
reserves—United States—Addresses, essays, lectures.
5.   United States—Forest policy—Addresses, essays,
lectures.   I.   Title.   II.   Series.
SD143.C55   333.7′5′0973   76-46999
ISBN 0-295-95540-6

THE GEO. S. LONG PUBLICATION SERIES

The Geo. S. Long Fund was established in 1975 to pro-
mote a better understanding of forestry, natural resources, and conservation. The endowment was made
by Miss Helen Long of Tacoma to the University of
Washington in memory of her father, a distinguished
timber industry executive and natural resources conservationist, who opened the first Weyerhaeuser office in
Tacoma in 1900 and served as the firm's manager, vice
president, and chairman of the executive committee.

The generous financial support provides an income to
the University of Washington to carry out the intent of
the founder with provisions that allow the dean of the
College of Forest Resources to administer a program of
lectures, publications, travel and literary acquisition.

The establishment of the lecture series with the intro-
duction of distinguished authorities to the academic and
forestry community has been endorsed by Miss Long as
a principal effort of the Fund. Publication of the Long
Lecturers as well as other educators and scientists in
associated disciplines will supplement and extend the
influence of the program. The present volume is comprised of three Walker-Ames Lectures.

The terms of the gift are broad enough to allow the
university to pursue scholarly excellence in such areas as

D. HIDEN RAMSEY LIBRARY
U. N. C. AT ASHEVILLE
ASHEVILLE, N. C.

special collections and the attendance of faculty at academic and professional meetings of special merit.

Seventy-five years elapsed between the time Geo. S. Long first arrived in the Pacific Northwest and the establishment of this series. With Miss Long's authorization and support the university will continue the legacy to work for a better understanding of forestry, natural resources, and conservation through academic efforts, a distinguished lecture series, and in this book.

Preface

THE three essays included herein were originally given as three public lectures at the University of Washington in April 1976, when I was serving as a Walker-Ames professor at that university. The audience for the Walker-Ames lectures was the general university public, and the essays are aimed at intelligent, serious, but nontechnical readers. The purpose of the lectures is to inform and, hopefully, to stimulate thought. They are not advocative of policies or viewpoints.

The first of the essays, "Land Use Planning and Land Use Control," deals with all types of land, in all ownerships, in all parts of the United States. It traces, in very broad outlines, the history of land use planning and land use controls in the United States. The rationale of public controls over private land use is considered, as are some of the mechanisms for such control. The divergences of interest among various private groups concerned with land use are explored. Finally, the possibilities of national land use legislation are described. My thought in putting this lecture first was to present a broad historical, philosophical background for the consideration of more specific land use issues.

The second essay, "Forests for Whom and for What?" is concerned with a particular kind of land—forested land; but with forests in all ownerships and in all parts of the United States. Some of the special characteristics and special problems of forests are described, as are the various uses and users groups of forests. A scheme of analysis for forest policy issues is presented and discussed in some detail. This essay gets down, a little more specifically, to the practical problems in the use of one kind of land—a kind of land very common and highly important in the Pacific Northwest. Enough theory and detail is presented, I hope, so that persons unfamiliar with forests will understand some of the special aspects of this kind of land, but not so much nor such technical detail as to repel the nonspecialist.

The third essay, "National Forests, Now and for the Future," focuses more narrowly on forests in this kind of federal ownership. Somewhat more detail particularly applicable to the Pacific Northwest is presented. The approach in this essay is rather different than most writing about national forests; it considers them from an economic viewpoint, not from a conservation, ecological, or silvicultural view. The conclusion reached is that the national forests produce many valuable goods and services but far less than their biological and economic potential. The possibility is raised that these forests are not managed as well, from an economic viewpoint, as they could be and should be. Specific data to support this view are included.

The ideas, the data, and even the methods of expression in these three essays have evolved over some years, as I have pursued my research, writing, and speaking. I would be hard pressed to try to recall when some particular idea first came to me, or from whom I got a particular stimulus, or when I first began to try to express some of the ideas herein. To a large extent, these essays are the summation or the distillation of such research and thinking over a considerable period of time. A harsh critic might say, with some accuracy, that I have previously said much of what is included here; but I hope that the careful distillation and the arrangement of facts and ideas here will prove informative, interesting, and even novel to readers.

In any writing, but especially in the kind of writing presented here, an author is indebted to a great many persons. First of all, I must acknowledge my considerable debt to the devoted men and women of the United States Forest Serivce, upon whose data and analyses we all depend. I am at times critical of the Forest Service, but I am always dependent upon it too. I wish also to acknowledge, without naming individuals, my many colleagues at Resources for the Future, in Washington, D.C., to whose stimulation and professional companionship I owe much of my own professional accomplishment. For many years they have provided an intellectual atmosphere that has been absolutely essential for my creative thought and writing. In recent years, as I have concentrated on forestry, I have learned a great deal from many of my professional forester friends. As one of them said once, "We will make you into a forester yet"; and if I have some competence in the technical and economic aspects of forestry, it is to them that I owe it. Lastly, I must acknowledge my debts to several most helpful persons at the University of Washington: to Dean James S. Bethel of the College of Forest Resources; to Thomas R. Waggener, associate professor in the same college, who did so much to arrange my schedule and to make life pleasant for me while I was at

the university; to David P. Thomas, of the same college;
to Dean Morgan D. Thomas, of the Graduate School,
and to Mrs. Valerie Smith of that School; and, lastly but
far from least, to the helpful people at the University of
Washington Press. None of these persons is, of course,
responsible for the views expressed or the errors I may
have made.

MARION CLAWSON

August 1976
Bethesda, Maryland

Contents

MAN, LAND, AND THE FOREST ENVIRONMENT

Land Use Planning
and Land Use Control

FOR more than 350 years the dominant situation in land use planning and control in the United States has been the interplay between the private developmental thrust and social controls over private land use.

The private developmental push began with a handful of tiny colonies along the Atlantic Coast and continued with relatively little intervention until the whole mid–North American continent had been settled. Private developers cleared forests to make farms, built towns and cities, constructed and operated factories, and built railroads. Private development continues to be a powerful economic, social, and political force and is responsible in no small part for the relatively high levels of living in the United States today. One basic ingredient of this developmental thrust has been private property rights for land: the right to own, to bequeath as one chooses, to use as one sees fit, and even to abuse with only a minimum of interference from others.

But, from the very beginning of settlement in what is now the United States, social controls established the framework within which private development could proceed. The very first step in private development was transfer of title from some king, landed proprietor, governor, federal or state government to some private individual or company. The social controls over private land which had been imported from the mother countries were gradually relaxed during the colonial and early national periods to a low point in the mid–nineteenth century. But they were never absent. By 1870 or thereabouts, a landowner could do almost anything he chose with his land, subject to relatively ineffectual laws of nuisance and other weak controls. Typically he owned mineral as well as surface rights, from the center of the earth to the zenith of the sky.

I refer throughout this book to social controls over private land use rather than to governmental controls. Most social controls, it is true, take the form of laws, regulations, and governmental programs. But there are two reasons why I prefer "social" to "governmental." First of all, in the United States, governments have powers only as derived from the people; governmental programs without popular support either do not survive or are ineffectual. Second, there have been social controls over land use which were not governmental. The early New England towns, for example, had land use patterns that were determined socially but not governmentally. Today, private lenders may dominate certain types of land use more than do any governmental agencies or programs. The extensive public use of private as well as of public forests for outdoor recreation is a form of social control over land use. Thus, as I see it, "social" is more inclusive and more basic than "governmental."

RURAL BEGINNINGS

The first modern social controls over private land use

were applied to farmland, not to the urban land uses that so much concern us today. Fence laws to restrict livestock and to protect crops from livestock were an early, and controversial, social control over private land use. Weed control laws were another. If a farmer did not undertake specified weed control measures, the local authorities moved onto his land and did it for him, at his expense. Drainage district laws brought drainage to a farmer's land, whether he wanted it or not, and made him pay his share of the cost of the group undertaking. Likewise, irrigation district laws levied charges against land within district boundaries, whether or not the farmer used water. All these forms of rural land use control were operative somewhere within the United States before 1900.

These social controls over rural land uses were not, so far as I can ascertain, the legal ancestors of social controls over urban land use. Their significance for us today lies in the fact that pragmatic legislators, often farmer-oriented and typically highly conservative in the original political sense, were willing to impose severe constraints on private land use when the situation really required it. Given the demonstrated necessity for strong social action, many men and organizations will accept measures to which they are philosophically opposed. The corollary, important to us today, is that many, probably most, people oppose social controls when the need for them is less clearly evident.

LAND USE CONTROLS SHIFT TO CITIES

The modern panoply of urban land use controls effectively began in New York City about the time of World War I, when Fifth-Avenue merchants sought to repel the clothing industry and its labor force from invading their aristocratic shopping and residential area. Within a decade, hundreds of cities and towns had zoning ordinances. The federal government, under the personal leadership of then Secretary of Commerce Herbert Hoover, developed a model zoning ordinance. Zoning as a form of social control over private land use was upheld by the Supreme Court in 1926 in the *Village of Euclid v. Ambler Realty Co.* case. More or less contemporaneously, other forms of social control, to which less publicity has usually been attached, were developed and applied. Subdivision regulations, building codes, health codes, and others exerted control over land uses in at least some situations.

Social controls over private land use and powerful social influences short of control have proliferated since the Depression and World War II. Federal funds of many kinds have provided financing for state and local land use planning. Highway funds, water pollution control funds, flood protection expenditures, public guarantee of private residential mortgages, urban renewal expenditures, soil conservation and farm improvement subsidies, and other forms of federal financial aid have greatly affected private land use. Local planning, zoning, subdivision, and other controls have become more numerous, more specific and limiting in their effect, and more likely to be effectively enforced. Federal environmental protection legislation of the last decade has had some effect on private land use and has the potential for vastly greater effects. Tax laws—federal, state, and local—have an increasing effect upon private land use.

SOCIAL CONTROLS AND PRIVATE LAND MARKETS

Social controls over private land use are more or less deliberate rejections of the free private market in land and the way it allocates land among different kinds of use and users. Private markets in land rarely meet the economists' ideal of the competitive market. The "commodity" is not standardized because every tract of land has some distinct characteristics. Buyers and sellers are often ill-informed and thus many choices are made that would be irrational if facts were better known. Typically at any given moment only a few potential buyers and a few potential sellers are actually in the market. In spite of these limitations, the private market could, and would if unfettered, allocate land by use and to user. However, there is a widespread conviction that important social objectives cannot be attained through the unregulated private market. Some may argue that this conviction is misplaced. I think not, but I do not intend to argue the matter here. Few, I think, can deny that such a public commitment to social controls over private land use exists and that the uncontrolled private market has been rejected as the sole determinant of land use.

In recent years, the conservation aspects of private land ownership have been the subject of a good bit of ill-informed discussion. Assertions that land or other resources owned in common will be excessively used and depleted and that privately owned land will be conserved and maintained do not rest on historical or geographic experience, nor are they necessarily true. Unregulated common resources are indeed likely to be misused, but the record shows that social controls have conserved forests, grazing lands, croplands, game, and

other resources in many situations. At the same time, a
private operation that correctly balances future income
streams and present realizable liquidation values may
well lead to sharp overuse and depletion. Social controls
can be fully as effective as private profit motives; either
may be soundly based on realities of resource characteristics, or either may be erroneous and ill-conceived.

ETHICAL BASIS OF SOCIAL CONTROL
OVER PRIVATE LAND USE

How, in fairness and justice, can society prevent a private landowner from using his land as he sees fit? Is not
the very essence of private property the right to exclude
others, so that the owner may enjoy his property as he
chooses? It may be argued that the value of the owner's
property is enhanced by the limitations society places on
all private lands in the locality, in the same sense that
every driver gains if all drivers are restricted to driving
on the right side of the road. But it remains true that
each landowner would gain if he could use his land as he
pleased while others were limited in their use of their
land.

In my view, the equity of social control over private
land use rests on four somewhat overlapping considerations: externalities, interdependencies, efficiency,
and environmental effects.

The concept of externalities in land (and other
natural resource) use has entered both professional and
popular literature in recent years. If one landowner
takes actions, the consequences of his actions affect
others who were not parties to the decision. Most attention has been focused on negative externalities, whereby
the other parties suffer losses or damages that the

decision-maker escapes. But positive externalities exist also, whereby the other parties gain benefits they do not pay for. An extensive legal history and an extensive economic literature has grown up on externalities.

The concept of externalities may be broadened to include interdependencies. Externalities imply and sometimes are described as an actor and recipient model, with the value stream, whether positive or negative, flowing one way. Interdependencies more realistically consider reciprocal value flows. Each landowner is part of the physical, social, and economic environment of every other landowner. These relationships, although they exist for all properties, are closer when properties are near one another. The value and use of any tract of land in the United States today depends more upon human actions elsewhere then it does upon anything that is or can be done on that specific tract. If anyone doubts this assertion, let him or her imagine a high tight fence around any property, through which neither persons nor goods could pass. The ability to buy inputs and the ability to sell outputs is critical to land use and value.

I do have a legitimate interest in how you use your land, for your actions affect me. Equally, you have a legitimate interest in how I use my land. The interrelations in land use are but one aspect of the complex web of physical, biological, economic, social, and political relations that characterize our modern world. There is every reason to expect these interrelations to grow in number and in strength as our population increases, as our technologies grow more complex, and as our economic output rises. To assert mutual interdependence does not, of course, justify every conceivable social control over private land use. On the contrary, the task of social engineering is to find or to devise those minimum controls over private land use which effectively and efficiently protect persons other than the decision-maker in each land use situation.

The efficiency argument for social controls over private land use has not been developed as fully as the argument based on externalities. The equitable basis for the compulsions inherent in drainage and irrigation district laws was not developed, so far as I have been able to ascertain, on efficiency grounds, although it might have been. It would be very costly (and sometimes well nigh impossible) to drain or to irrigate only certain tracts while leaving islands of undrained or unirrigated land. Substantial areas of land, often comprised of scores or hundreds of ownership tracts, must be treated as units. If the majority of landowners want to drain or to irrigate, the dissenting minority must, at the least, pay its share of costs and, in the case of drainage, participate in the action even when the landowner would prefer not to do so.

The efficiency argument applies equally to many urban and suburban situations. It would be very costly to build a superhighway or a throughway for only a few land users; the minimum capacity of a certain type of road requires the occupiers of substantial areas of land to make use of the facility. The same is true of sewer lines. A line installed to serve one subdivision would not only be costly but uneconomic as well, since lines usually have the capacity to serve additional areas. The economies of scale for many modern services such as roads and sewer lines are substantial. Unfortunately, such potential social controls over private land use as the location, timing, and pricing of public services have generally not been used. Postage-stamp pricing over wide areas destroys a major potential land use control. If the developer or residents of a new subdivision had to pay the full cost of sewers, for example, this charge would offset the savings on land that encouraged the leap-frog development. As governmental budgets grow tighter and as some natural resources (such as energy) grow more expensive, efficiency considerations in social control over private land use are likely to become more important.

The fourth equitable base for social control over private land use is one of environmental considerations. To a substantial degree, but not wholly, these considerations are included with the externalities and interdependencies. As a society we forbid the dumping of some wastes into streams or into the air; this may be justified on the basis of preventing damages to other landowners or water users (externality) or on the grounds of environmental protection. But some types of social controls over private land use have an environmental base where externalities are either absent or inconsequential. For instance, in many political jurisdictions septic tanks are forbidden for health reasons, to protect the property owner more than to protect his neighbors. Health codes may likewise forbid certain kinds of building use, again to protect the occupants more than to protect others. More commonly, however, environmental considerations involve externalities.

The meaning of such words as *equity* and *justice*, in actual application, have changed over the decades and are likely to continue to change in future decades. What the body politic considers fair and reasonable is a function of the age; what was once unacceptable may not be so today or tomorrow. The courts, too, have changed their definitions, although always with a lag behind developing social thought and social conscience. Some fifty years ago, land use zoning was a daring innovation just receiving judicial blessing. Today, similar zoning is being struck down because it does not provide for the reasonable needs of people who would like to reside in the area but are effectively prevented from doing so by land use ordinances. As our society and economy change, our concepts of equity and fairness will almost surely change also. I think it highly probable that social controls over private land use will increase in number and severity and that they will be defended on the grounds of equity and justice.

DIVERGENCES OF INTEREST

Land use planning and land use controls, to the extent they are effective in practice, not only reveal divergences of interest among many groups but sometimes intensify them.

Some current popular or nontechnical writing about land use planning and land use controls seems to assume that a particular course of action is so eminently reasonable and sensible that each and every enlightened citizen will accept it. Aside from the fact that unanimity rarely exists on any issue among groups of any real size, the history of land use in any locality should disabuse the perceptive observer of notions about unanimity in the land use field. Careful planning and wise social engineering may reduce divergences of interest or may offer alternative rewards to losers in the land control process, but some hard core of disagreement over land use is likely to remain. To proceed as if this were not true may be folly.

The divergences of interest over land use controls may be broadly grouped into those within a community (however defined) and those between a community and outsiders. Each of these in turn has other characteristics.

Within a community, especially within a suburban community, there is often a divergence between residential and nonresidential (business or service) land uses. The typical homeowner fights to preserve the character of his neighborhood, as he perceives it. He was drawn to the community by this residential character, often has substantial emotional commitment to it, and fights to prevent its loss. A proposal to extend the business district into, or even toward, the residential area will be strongly opposed by its residents. A proposal actually to establish a business, such as a service station, clearly within the residential community will provoke even stronger opposition.

The business–residential divergence of interest is closely paralleled by the development–preservation or the profit–amenity divergence. Proposals to develop certain tracts of land, particularly those of certain physical types such as swamps, often arouse a substantial popular opposition. People who do not own the land in question, bear no part of the costs of its ownership and maintenance, and often do not actually use it in any physical sense, nevertheless feel strongly that it should be maintained in its undeveloped condition. Similar controversy arises over structures that have, or are alleged to have, unusual architectural quality and/or important historical values. A proposal to tear down one of these structures will typically arouse much vocal opposition.

Another closely related divergence of interest occurs between environmental protection and economic development or activity. Most actual or potential land users will at least pay lip service to the principle of environmental protection these days, but disagreement arises over such specifics as the severity (and hence the costliness) of the controls and the land use activities to be excluded or severely restricted in particular situations. The issue often arises sharply when a new environmental protection law prohibits a long-established local business from carrying on as it has in the past and significant numbers of jobs within the community seem to be threatened.

Land use interests may also diverge over what types of housing ought to be built on a specific area. In particular, a proposal to construct an apartment building or complex in or adjacent to a community of single family homes will almost certainly set off a local controversy, especially if the homes are relatively highly valued. Proposals for rezoning will be strongly opposed. Analyses will be presented by the homeowners seeking to prove that the apartment residents will demand more governmental services than the taxes on the apartment will support. The developers will seek to show the reverse. Invidious comparisons between the anticipated new renters and the established owners will be made. And whatever the outcome, furor and emotionalism will almost certainly characterize the proceedings.

In many of the conflicts of interest over local land use planning and land use control, the lines are distinctly drawn between rich and poor, or at least between the upper-middle and lower-middle classes.

In some instances an individual gets caught in two or

more incompatable personal roles within the community. As an upper-class resident and conservationist, Mr. X wishes to preserve unchanged the character of his residential area, wants strict environmental controls, and desires the preservation of some natural area. But as a businessman, he wants a location for his business, "reasonable" environmental controls, and suitable nearby housing for his employees. Innumerable other combinations of personal interest positions are, of course, possible.

Most of these intracommunity divergences of interest in land use planning and land use control have their counterpart in divergence of interest between the community and outsiders. In addition, some divergences are peculiar to, or are more marked in, the community–outsider divergences. Much depends upon how tightly the community is defined and bounded. The small residential suburb or subdivision, composed of single family homes, may have comparatively few intracommunity divergences and comparatively many community vs outsider divergences, for instance.

Many local governments have consciously used land use controls as a weapon of class interest against outsiders. They have excluded or imposed severe restrictions on apartments, rental residential properties, and new housing within the economic capacity of the low-income population. These actions have been aimed at the poor in general, at people of different lifestyles, and at undesired racial and ethnic groups, regardless of their income. This type of exclusionary land use planning and land use control is under increasingly heavy legal attack. But it is far from obsolete yet.

A critical social policy issue in this divergence of interest between community and outsider in land use planning and land use control is whether "community" for purposes of legal process shall be defined in larger and more inclusive terms than "community" for local self-government. In particular, who has a right to challenge local land use controls? Who has standing in court? Must one be a property owner within the community who can contend that his property values have been diminished by some governmental action, or may he be the representative of a class of people who would be or might be residents of the community if land use controls were to be changed? With typical steps forward, backward, and sideways courts are wrestling with these problems. The cozy exclusiveness of the high-income suburb is surely threatened. The courts are likely to view land use actions in a broader context and consider the impact on the metropolitan area as a whole, or on an even larger area. Zoning against apartments, for instance, may no longer be regarded as a purely local land use action.

WHO CONTROLS LAND USE? AND HOW?

The growing complexity of technological, economic, and social interrelationships in the United States will surely support the evident trend toward more and stricter social controls over private land use in the future. The real issue of public policy is not whether to have more social controls over private land use; that issue has already been decided. The real questions today are: On what basis shall such controls be exercised? In what form? Who is to make decisions, and who is to enforce them? Can democratic processes to protect minority rights be established and maintained?

These general and somewhat abstract ideas are more

readily comprehensible if we reduce them to more personalized situations. Every homeowner is anxious to maintain the quality of his neighborhood, as every merchant is anxious to retain the character of his business area. Each is willing to support some measures of control on the land uses of other persons, to the end that the local area shall not be changed adversely. Each can see the rationale and the equity of such land use controls, because everyone benefits from the restrictions on a few persons.

But how far are we each willing to submit to controls that are imposed by others on how we may use our land? If we wish to install an apartment arrangement in our house so that aged parents may live with us on a somewhat private basis, but the local zoning ordinance says "no second family in a one-family house," then how do we feel? Are we prepared to allow others to control the use of our land and property, in the name of community values, which we would like to exercise over the use of their land? In the words of the ancient query, whose ox is being gored by whose bull?

It is precisely in the ambivalence between what the average property owner perceives as reasonable when applied to others and what he is willing to accept when applied to himself that much of the conflict and uncertainty about land use planning and land use controls arises and continues.

A long held and not yet entirely abandoned myth of land use planning is that objective study or the application of "scientific" principles would somehow lead to the discovery or invention of the one best land use pattern. Experience has shown that objective facts can indeed be useful for land use planning. Physical, biological, economic, social, and political data of many kinds can help to define and even to evaluate alternatives. Furthermore, the use of the best professional expertise eliminates many alternatives as infeasible, too costly, or in some way unacceptable. But land use planning is not, and never can be, a mechanical process that is reducible to an equation and capable of computer programming. At numerous points, uncertainties about future facts and future relationships require decisions or choices that are often unavoidably subjective in character. Still more important, there is not a single best answer, but a variety of possible answers, each acceptable to a different group of citizens.

One hopes that land use planning and land use controls in the future will be based upon a combination of the best objective information available, the best professional judgments possible, and the active participation of citizen groups. Land use planning and control are not only too complex to be left to the enthusiastic part-time amateur but have too serious an effect on the average citizen to be left to the professional planner alone. An effective blending of professional expertise and citizen involvement is to be sought. The reality may be far short of the ideal, of course, but the ideal is unlikely to be achieved unless we know what we seek.

Land use planning and social control over private land use are inevitably a political process. Instead of decrying this fact, as so many people do, we should be glad it is true, and seek to make the political process work as well as possible. We should by all means inventory facts, make analyses, and develop alternatives as accurately and as objectively as possible. The political process should not enter at these stages. But once the alternatives have been identified, the political process should take over and make the choices, especially as to instruments and methods of control. I do not favor giving the professional land use planner the legal power to "adopt" a land use plan. Rather, I feel that formal or legal approval should be made by a body representing the whole electorate of the area. Despite its shortcomings, a democratically elected government most nearly achieves the wishes and desires of the citizenry.

At every stage in the planning process, two-way communication between planner and citizen can and should be fostered. Modern technology offers many possibilities for communication. Open meetings of planning bodies to receive the reactions of citizens and citizen groups are essential. The formal public hearing and the formal appeals process are indispensable parts of the process.

Land use planning and control over private land use in the past has all too often been class-oriented in its effects, and in some instances, in its intent. One would hope this would be less true in the future. The ability of minority groups to make themselves heard will surely affect much land use planning in the future. So will the attitude of the courts if they reject land use controls that adversely and unfairly affect various social classes and minority groups. Land use planning will always directly involve a community's leaders more than its ordinary voters, but surely leaders from more varied backgrounds can be involved in the future.

Social controls over private land use must inevitably restrain some citizens from using their land as they would in the absence of controls. Unless controls restrain someone, they are worthless. Their function is not simply one of allocating land among alternative uses, because, as noted earlier, the private market can achieve this on its own. Social controls, to have a purpose, must seek some other result.

As I have said on several occasions, a land use control is not worth having unless it bites someone. The questions are, whom to bite, how hard, and with what risk that he bites back? Many land planners have sought to exercise social controls over private land use, only to have the controls rejected and the planning body damaged or even destroyed by the opposition. Private opposition to social control over land use should be expected. Its absence would almost surely signify that the proposed controls were worthless. If the planning and political processes outlined above are followed, social controls over private land use are likely to become both more efficient by achieving desired purposes with minimum controls and more effective in winning the acceptance of the electorate, legislature, and courts.

Land use planning and land use control are forms of social engineering. The optimum solution is one that is accepted by most people, actively supported by many, and strongly opposed by only a few. Professional planners and other specialists should lead popular thinking, but not get so far ahead of it that they lose their followers. What is acceptable today may be old stuff tomorrow; and what is unacceptable today may be acceptable tomorrow. As times change, so do social attitudes. And, although some of the hard facts that enter into land use planning (soil types and topography, for instance) may be well-nigh unchangeable, the way these facts condition land use may also change with time.

Land use planning and social control over private

land use in the United States have mostly been functions of local government—cities, counties, and special districts. The states, from which these units of government gained their land control power, gave relatively little attention to the matter until about a decade ago. The federal government, also until a decade ago, exercised little direct control over private land use, although many of its programs had substantial influence over private land use. To a significant extent, this situation is changing. The federal government is increasingly exercising direct control over private land use, by such means as coastal zone, water pollution, and air-quality legislation. Its grants-in-aid to states and local government for land use planning are substantial incentives. Its typical requirement of a "comprehensive land use plan" as a condition of transportation, public housing, sewer, and other subsidies has had a pronounced effect upon state and local action.

But states are also getting more directly involved in the land use planning and land use control business. A half-dozen states, including Vermont, Florida, California, and others, have set up mechanisms for direct control of private land use in some situations or for some uses. Several states are beginning to exercise a degree of supervision over the powers they delegated to local governments, and proposals to this end have been made by governors or legislators in other states.

The courts have been challenging the localism and the exclusionary tactics of local government in land use controls. A suburb, a city, or a county that seeks to repel more residents or residents of certain economic and social classes may find itself subject to challenge. A well-conceived and factually supported plan to control the pace of growth may be sustained when a simple prohibition against any growth or against certain forms of growth would be stricken down.

The end results of these shifting centers of political power over land use planning and control are not easily predictable. A new federalism is emerging for this general field of government. Like all existing federalisms, power will be distributed among levels and units of government in ways that seem illogical to the stranger, yet seem to work, often very well. Land use planning should be a particularly interesting field for the student of American government to watch during the next few decades.

NATIONAL LAND USE LEGISLATION

Proposals for national land use legislation have appeared repeatedly over the past decade or longer, but were largely ignored by the Congress until about five years ago. Congressional interest at that time aroused an early optimism that a national land use law would soon be passed. This rather naïve optimism has been effectively chilled by the passage of time. Faith in the belief that national land use legislation can resolve conflicts over land use has shown more survival power, but in the end it, too, may be eroded.

Even a casual survey of local land use planning in the United States reveals many inconsistencies in planning practices, as well as many actions that are dubious or worse in terms of due legal process, good governmental practice, and protection of the rights of various classes of the society. In addition, the lack of generally accepted plans has often led to wasteful duplications or discrepancies in governmental programs. Faced with the evident shortcomings of local land use planning, many persons have suggested some degree of national direction or national land use planning. Even the most ardent advocates of national leadership have shied away from direct federal involvement in what are basically local land use problems. The problem of attempting to deal with myriad local situations and the almost certain political opposition to direct planning by the federal government have led to proposals for a certain degree of national guidance and some amount of federal financial aid, but with land use planning powers still largely in the hands of the states and local governments. The goal of effective yet fair national leadership has not yet been achieved.

The Congress has shown a notable lack of enthusiasm for strong national land use legislation. Attempts to pass any bill through both Senate and House have failed repeatedly, as even the casual newspaper reader knows. What is less well known is the fact that successive drafts have been watered down substantially. When the bill sponsored by Senator Henry M. Jackson of Washington came before the Senate in late summer 1971 it contained significant penalties against states that failed to meet some very general and undemanding land use planning standards. Those penalties were amended out of the bill by Senate vote. The bill, by intention (I presume), set no policy guidelines for states in their land use planning; Senator Edmund G. Muskie of Maine and other senators failed to persuade the Senate to adopt amendments restating national policies (such as pollution control) that had become law in earlier legislation. The rejection of strong land use legislation at this time was an early sign of the mood of the Senate.

Nearly two years later the Senate did pass a milder bill, but when the House seemed on the verge of passing it, Congressman Sam Steiger of Arizona prevailed upon President Nixon to repudiate previous administration support. Steiger was able to capitalize on the President's urgent need at that moment for House support in his anticipated impeachment fight, and the bill was not passed. Land use legislation was the victim of unfortunate timing: six months earlier, Nixon saw no need to curry support from conservative Republicans, and six months later he was gone from the White House. Contributing to Steiger's success was the substantial degree of fear, suspicion, and distrust throughout the country of the possible or probable effects of national land use legislation. Proponents of the legislation could argue that such fears were unwarranted, but many people were seriously concerned.

This brief account of recent legislative history is proof, if proof is needed, that passage of national land use legislation is a difficult matter. At least two major problems exist. The first is occasioned by divergence of interest discussed previously and by the fear of outside control. To many people, local land use planning and control is bad enough, even when they feel they can influence it and see that it has no real teeth. State or federal control, in the hands of possibly hostile groups, is another matter altogether. The second major problem is rooted in the enormous diversity of land use situations in the United States, which makes it virtually impossible to write legislation that will not be foolish, harmful, or irrelevant in some land use situation.

Most proponents of federal land use legislation seem not to realize that two fairly ambitious efforts at national land use planning were undertaken during the 1930's. The National Resources Planning Board undertook one kind of national land use planning, and the United States Department of Agriculture undertook another. I will not give a detailed review of either, but both were ended by explicit action of Congress, which rebelled against each. While many factors were involved, in each case the planners got too far "ahead" or at least out of touch with too large and too powerful a segment of their constituency. Sometimes, making haste slowly accomplishes more than more ambitious drives.

My judgment is that a national land use act will be passed some day, but surely not in 1976, and probably not in 1977 (the new administration will have more urgent concerns), but in some unpredictable later year. It will almost surely be a "weak" act, dealing with procedure and not explicitly with policy, making rather small grants to states and local government, and lacking any real penalties for noncompliance. My further judgment is that, whatever the original terms may be, the act will be substantially amended within five years as experience accumulates. I do not wholly rule out the possibility of repeal in that time frame.

Would a "weak" act be worth having? Would it accomplish anything significant? As a student of national land use policy, I would accept a fairly weak act, in part because I think nothing else can be passed and in part because I think many areas and many groups need to learn to walk before they attempt to run. Even the weakest bills that have been seriously considered to date would have provided some encouragement to states and local government to undertake more and better land use planning. The accomplishments of a weak act may not be great, but there may at least be more uniformity in planning processes and in land use control measures. There will be nothing in any federal legislation, I am sure, that will inhibit or prevent any state, city, or county from going as far and as fast in land use planning and control as it chooses or is able to go.

The easy optimism and simple faith in national land use legislation of the recent past may be replaced by a more sober, realistic, achievable program of action.

Forests for Whom and for What?

FORESTS are important in the total American landscape, in the natural resource base of our economy, and in the economic and social life of the people. The importance of forests tends generally to be underestimated in the United States, but is better understood in the Pacific Northwest than almost anywhere else in the country.

Forests of one kind or another today occupy one third of the land in the fifty states. About a third of the total forest area is classed as "noncommercial" in the usual forest statistics, because its timber stand per acre is too low, or its potential for growing wood annually is too small, or for some other reason. Much of the noncommercial forest is in the interior of Alaska where annual wood growth per acre is low. In my judgment, repeatedly expressed, about one-fourth of the forest area classified as commercial is actually incapable of continued economic wood production. By any reasonable accounting, however, there remains a substantial acreage of commercial forest.

The United States has many kinds of forests and, in my estimate, some four thousand significantly different forest management situations. There are about a score of major forest types, well over one hundred important commercial tree species, a dozen important regionally distinct forest situations, and at least four major kinds of forest ownerships. In addition, forest sites differ greatly in productivity, and present forest stands differ in degree of stocking, age of trees, freedom from disease, and other factors.

One can generalize about forests in the same sense that one can generalize about farms, lakes, cities, or schools. But for many purposes, it is highly important to specify the kind of forest under discussion because what is true of one forest may not be true of another. In this chapter, I speak about forests as a whole; my third chapter concentrates on the national forests.

The forested acreage in the United States today is considerably smaller than it was when the first colonists arrived from Europe. But in recent years forests have become re-established on millions of acres that were once cleared, as they had to be if cultivated crops were to be grown and if towns and roads were to be built. To the first settlers the forests were often a nuisance, something to be gotten rid of. For over one hundred years, and especially in the past fifty years, trees have been invading abandoned cropland, notably along the Atlantic Coast, especially in hilly and mountainous areas, but also in parts of the coastal plain and Piedmont.

Trees grow "naturally" in much of the United States. That is, in the absence of man's efforts to prevent tree growth by such means as annual plowing or mowing, trees of some species will invade the land. Many tree species are aggressive and persistent invaders on any land where they are not firmly suppressed. The resultant growth may not be productive forest, and the initial invading species may be replaced in a few years by other species, but the land surface quickly becomes covered with trees in these extensive naturally forested regions.

The capacity of trees to grow, in spite of man's efforts to keep them out or in the face of his neglect of the land, has been grossly and repeatedly underestimated. Cries of timber famine have been heard over the years when someone noted that timber harvest had removed tree cover, and then projected that rate of removal some years ahead without considering probable tree growth. Gifford Pinchot and T. R. Roosevelt did this shortly after the turn of the century. Others foresaw economic decline as old-growth timber was harvested in the 1920s and 1930s, and modern "conservationists" have been greatly disturbed at timber harvest. All of them grossly underestimated the capacity of trees to become re-established. I do not mean to say that timber harvest and forest management practices have been fully satisfactory. On the contrary, there was much waste and little forethought for the future. But no one should underestimate the recuperative capacity of any ecosystem, especially of forests on sites well-suited for tree growth.

FORESTS PRODUCE MANY OUTPUTS

Foresters have long emphasized that forests produce many kinds of outputs. First and most obvious, of course, is wood. Trees, like all living matter, have a finite life cycle. The tree starts with a seed that sprouts to become a seedling, and then passes through the sapling and pole stages into adulthood, and, if unharvested, ultimately declines and dies. The casual observer seeing a forest annually or at other relatively short intervals may be unaware of the life-cycle changes that are typically spread over several decades. No tree can be kept alive and growing forever; even those antiquarians, the

Sequoia gigantea and the bristle cone pine, ultimately die. Forests, like cultivated crops, grow at widely varying rates on different sites.

Forests also serve as rather special watersheds. Every area that supports a commercial forest has at least a fair amount of annual precipitation. The trees protect the surface of the land from erosion; intercept some of the rain or snow, which evaporates before it hits ground; and consume large amounts of soil moisture from both deep and shallow layers of the soil. In general, forests are an excellent kind of watershed, and their extensive area makes them especially important in the United States.

Wildlife is also a forest output. The edges of the forest and the forest clearings, in particular, offer food, shelter, and breeding areas for many kinds of wildlife.

Many people seek outdoor recreation in a forest setting. A dense forest is often unattractive for outdoor recreation, but trees enhance the attractiveness of camping and picnicking recreation areas. The recreationist is often unaware and unconcerned about annual growth as long as the trees seem relatively healthy and attractive. He is also unlikely to be aware of how his activities can affect the forest. Overuse for outdoor recreation will produce adverse environmental impacts, just as will overuse for any other forest product.

A special form of recreation that has aroused much interest and controversy in recent years is wilderness use. *Wilderness* is a term of many meanings. In the broadest sense it refers to a kind of area and a kind of personal experience, although complete agreement exists on neither. Must each wilderness area be 100,000 acres in extent, as in the original Forest Service definition, or 5,000 acres as in the roadless areas now under consideration for wilderness classification, or may it be no more than 20 acres, as a private "mini-wilderness?" Must the wilderness user encounter no other persons, or are a few other wilderness visitors tolerable, or does the "wilderness" begin when the user steps off the edge of a blacktop road? Regardless of definition, a wilderness need not be a commercial forest. Indeed, about half the acreage of wilderness areas within national forests do not have commercial forests as these are conventionally defined. Some wilderness areas are above timber line or have very sparse stands of trees; some are lakes or swamps.

Another important, yet hard to describe, output of forests may best be called "a general forest environment." Even persons uninformed about forests and generally unappreciative of them will find a green forest a more pleasant site than bare land, burned-over areas, or weedy and brushy fields. Many people, of course, are well-informed and concerned about forests and are able to recognize and appreciate healthy, vigorous ones. Walking, riding, or driving through forests is satisfying to many people. Forests in this general environmental sense are as important as lawns, shrubs, and flowers in towns and cities on land never occupied by the observer.

WHO USES FORESTS?

Most people are unaware of how much they depend on forests for important everyday needs. Everyone uses wood, for instance, every day in some form. I have tried to imagine someone who used no wood. He or she would have to live in a cave, for all buildings use wood in some way, whether during the construction process or as part of the building. He or she would have to use stone furniture, for all other furniture is either made of wood or wood is used in the construction process. Coal picked up from the surface of the ground would have to constitute the sole fuel, for any other source of fuel requires wood at some point in the production process.

Most people, as they shop for foods or other items packaged (at least at some stage) in paper, or as they buy newspapers or magazines, or use any of the scores of other items common to ordinary day-to-day living, are unaware of their dependence on wood and wood fiber. They may be acutely conscious of the cost of these products, and would be greatly upset if such products were unavailable in stores, yet they do not make the connection between their needs and the forest.

Everyone uses water, of course, and the probabilities are very high that at least part of the water consumed fell to earth on a forested area. Again, the connection between the water flowing from the tap and the forested watershed from which it came is not apparent to the average urban dweller.

Perhaps half of the total population each year enjoys outdoor recreation in a forest setting. Some people do not participate in outdoor recreation because they are too old, too young, ill, or cannot afford to travel to recreation sites. Others could participate but choose not to. Most of the outdoor recreation in a forest setting is in publicly owned forests or parks, but much is on forest-industry forests, and many people own forested properties for their own enjoyment.

Forested wilderness areas are used by a relatively small part of the total population. Visitors to formally designated forested wilderness areas each year are less than 2 percent of the total population, and perhaps no more than 10 percent of the population ever visit such areas. A higher percentage of the population endorses the idea of wilderness and gets a certain satisfaction simply from knowing that such areas are there, but it is very difficult to estimate just how many people fall in this category.

Likewise, it is difficult to know how many people enjoy the general forest environment, or just how important this enjoyment may be to them, but intuitively one judges that their numbers are larger.

FORESTS ARE A RENEWABLE RESOURCE

Forests are a renewable resource. Plants growing within forests capture solar energy and transform it into products that man can use. Only a small part of the total solar energy is transformed into products, it is true, but no process other than photosynthesis utilizes so much of this energy so economically.

The renewability of forests is most often emphasized in connection with wood production. Even if forests are managed with no more than a minimum of competence, wood can be grown indefinitely on each forest area. All the substitutes for wood in construction, packaging, and other wood-fiber use are nonrenewable. In general, wood requires less energy for processing than do alternative materials. These important values of wood must, of course, be balanced against other factors in using wood and alternative materials.

Water is equally a renewable resource. From evaporation to precipitation to flow, the hydrologic cycle is powered by solar energy. An unforested area of land might yield as much or even more water than a forested area, but the water quality is likely to be inferior.

Forest services such as outdoor recreation, wilderness experiences, and wildlife production are all renewable resources too. Forests can produce these services indefinitely also.

Although forest outputs are renewable, they are also perishable. The wood grown one year may be harvested in any one of many future years, depending in part upon the species and the age of the tree. Once harvested, the wood will normally last for decades, although in the end it rots and decays. Most other forest outputs lie at the opposite end of the perishability scale. An outdoor recreation or wilderness opportunity not used this year—indeed, not used this day—cannot be stored for later use but is lost forever. Likewise, the stream flow unused by man one year (or day) may be lost for later use. Economic management of these "perishable" forest outputs requires some means for using them at the rate they are produced.

FOREST OWNERSHIP AND FOREST USES

Four major categories of forest ownership are recognized in much of the data about forests: national forests, other public forests, forest-industry forests, and "other" forests. Some of these major categories are often divided further. For instance, some of the other public forests are federally owned and managed by various federal agencies such as the Bureau of Land Management, the Tennessee Valley Authority, the Department of Defense, and others; and some are owned by states and counties. The "other" forests are owned by a mixed lot of private parties—some as parts of farms, some as incidental to other businesses, some for hobbies or personal recreation, and some primarily for speculative gains in price. To some extent, each kind of owner faces problems peculiar to his ownership class. But all forest owners, public and private, face certain problems more or less to the same extent.

One problem common to all forest ownership is how the owner can secure some economic return for valuable forest outputs that are generally not marketed for cash. Outdoor recreation, wilderness use, water, wildlife, and the general forest environment each has economic value, but in the American society those who enjoy these forest outputs rarely pay much or anything for them. Millions of people enjoy outdoor recreation activities on both publicly and privately owned forests, paying little or nothing for the privilege. The man who owns a tract of forest for his own enjoyment does indeed bear the costs of ownership, but often he is unable to prevent others from using his property without payment. Wilderness exists mostly on public land, and wilderness users pay little for their enjoyment of such areas. Except for a few municipal watersheds, water flowing from forested areas is free to users who have established water rights under applicable law. Only rarely does a forest owner collect anything for protecting wildlife.

The legal right of the forest owner to exclude those who do not pay for these forest outputs or to charge user fees is too complex an issue to be explored here. But the practical, social, and political obstacles to collecting any significant revenues at any reasonable administrative cost are well-nigh insurmountable. The average American seems to think he should enjoy many forests outputs without paying for them, and he shows little concern for the problems his use creates for the forest owner.

A few of the problems peculiar to each particular class of forest owners may be mentioned briefly. Public forests as a whole seem to suffer from two major problems: (1) a notable lack of clear legislative directives on how to manage these forests; and (2) tardy and inadequate annual appropriations for competent management. The "other" forests, mostly relatively small units the owners of which are technically untrained in forestry, often will not repay the time and effort needed for careful management. The owners cannot afford to own equipment or to maintain a permanent labor force, and often they find it difficult or impossible to carry out the forest practices they would like to employ.

COMPATIBLE AND INCOMPATIBLE FOREST USES

Three of the many uses or outputs of forests are basically incompatible with one another: wood production, wilderness, and outdoor recreation other than wilderness. Three other uses, however, are reasonably compatible with one another and with each of the three incompatibles. These are watershed, wildlife, and general forest environment.

Timber harvest destroys wilderness areas, and wilderness reservation makes timber harvest impossible. If one relaxes the standards of wilderness, something akin to the old wilderness may be recreated in fifty to one hundred years after timber harvest, if roads are closed and other uses are prohibited. But if one insists on virginity in his wilderness, then timber harvest is impossible forever.

Wilderness is equally incompatible with outdoor recreation of moderately intensive types. An access road, a picnic area, a campground, an intensive fishing area, and other recreation developments are fully as incompatible with a wilderness as are chain saws and logging trucks.

Moderately intensive outdoor recreation and wood production are primarily incompatible but not entirely so. Some forms of outdoor recreation, such as hunting, are facilitated by timber harvest, because game animals and birds increase on the cutover areas. Timber can be harvested on campgrounds on a selective basis or on a long rotation. Roads for timber harvest open up areas for outdoor recreation. Other compatibilities might be cited, but, on the whole, timber harvest and active outdoor recreation are largely incompatible.

In contrast, watershed, wildlife, and general forest environment are generally compatible with one another and with each of the three incompatibles. A properly planned and executed timber harvest will preserve the watershed and the forest environment and favor some wildlife while disadvantaging other kinds. Wilderness is generally favorable to each of these three compatible uses. Outdoor recreation can damage any of the three if it is too intensive, but when properly controlled it is not inimical to them.

The degree of compatibility or incompatibility is often affected by the forest type, the site classification of the land, and the stage in the tree-growing cycle. The general relationships suggested above may need modification for particular forest situations. In many instances, trade-offs are possible—a little less timber harvest for much more outdoor recreation, for instance. The im-

portant trade-off may not be between outputs, but between one input and another output—a little more
money spent on timber access roads to reduce damage
to the watershed, for instance.

A compatibility–incompatibility analysis is, in my
judgment, vastly more useful than sloganeering about
multiple use. If one interprets multiple use to mean that
every output is sought on every acre every year, then the
idea is absurd. If one interprets multiple use as a vari-
able combination of outputs on different tracts, so that
the larger area is managed for all feasible combinations
of outputs, then multiple use acquires a larger and more
practical meaning. In any case, the trade-offs between
one use and another are critical, and it is here that the
compatibility–incompatibility analysis is particularly useful.

POTENTIAL OF FORESTS TO SERVE PEOPLE

The gap between actual and potential output is
greater for forests than for any other natural resource
of the United States with which I am at all familiar. This
statement is generally true for each major kind of forest
ownership and for most specific forest situations. There
are exceptions, of course, and some forests are producing at or close to their economic potential. While forests
now contribute greatly to American life, they are capable of contributing much more. These general statements apply to all forest outputs—wood, outdoor recreation, wilderness, wildlife, water, and others; but the
data are best for wood, and the quantitative relationships can most easily be expressed for wood production.
In 1970 (the last year for which reasonably good data
are available) the forests of the United States were grow-

ing just half as much wood as fully stocked and reasonably well-managed natural stands of timber would
grow. The forest-industry forests achieved 59 percent of
their potential, but the national forests achieved only 39
percent of their potential. Intensive forest management,
if applied to all forests, could produce twice as much
wood annually as reasonably good natural stand management does.

Intensive forest management for wood production
will not pay on all forest sites or for some forest types.
On the less productive sites, the more remote sites, and
the sites where road-building and other harvest costs are
high, intensive management will return less than it costs.
Indeed, on some of these sites, even good natural stand
management may not pay. In addition to the economic
considerations, environmental concerns should elimi-
nate wood harvest, and hence wood growing, on excessively steep slopes, easily erodable soils, sites where tree
reproduction is uncertain or slow, and on the edge of
some water courses and water bodies. But, after full allowance for limiting production on such sites, annual
wood production from American forests could still be
fully double the current level.

I have not mentioned the limitation that wilderness
reservation would impose upon wood growing, because
much depends on how wilderness is defined. If a forest
wilderness continues to be defined as an area of at least
5000 roadless acres and no permanent human occu-
pancy, then wilderness offers little threat to wood growing. About half of the areas that meet these standards
have no commercial forest, and considerable parts of the
others should not be used for continued wood production for economic and environmental reasons.

The threat that wilderness advocates pose for wood production lies in two different directions. The first derives from the definition of wilderness. When the Forest Service first established wilderness areas by administrative action in the 1920s, 100,000 acres was considered the minimum unit; since the Wilderness Act was passed in 1964, areas of 5000 roadless acres have been studied for possible wilderness designation, and some much smaller areas have in fact been designated as wilderness. A further drastic lowering of minimum area would involve far larger acreages and far more valuable timber lands. It would also drastically lower the quality of the wilderness experience. The second threat to wood production, posed by the wilderness advocates as a group rather than by wilderness use as such, lies in the attempts to prescribe timber rotations, harvest methods, rates of cutting, and the like on areas fully capable of economic timber production. This latter type of activity is vastly more of a threat to wood growing than is any probable reservation of wilderness areas.

The acreage of land (some not forested) within national forests which meets present wilderness standards is three times, possibly more, the area presently so designated, In addition, the resource potential exists for the establishment of some "restored wildernesses" or some "quasi-wildernesses" on lands not federally owned, if wilderness users are prepared to pay the costs. Still further, the capacity of wilderness areas to accommodate visitors without significant loss in the quality of the wilderness experience could be increased greatly by the building of more trails into presently unused areas and by more careful scheduling of visitors on the trails.

The capacity of forests to provide outdoor recreation,

to serve as a home for wildlife to yield water, and to be an attractive part of the total natural environment far exceeds current production of each of these outputs. Through the application of modern technology, the investment of more capital and labor, and, above all, a higher level of management skills, the output of each of these forest services could be increased. The physical or biological potential for each service is greater than the economic potential, but even the latter is well above the present output.

The dominant, indeed, the dramatic, fact about forest potential is that the American people can have more of *everything* from the forests, if they but apply enough thought and effort. Over the past fifty years forests have indeed yielded more of everything—more wilderness use, more outdoor recreation of other kinds, more wildlife, and more wood. In particular situations and at particular times, more wood has meant less recreation, or other conflicts, and trade-offs have occurred. But for the forest system as a whole and over a significant period of time, all outputs can be increased.

ANALYSIS OF FOREST POLICY ISSUES

The management and the use of forests, both private and public, frequently pose important issues of policy. For the public forests, the public policy issues are inescapable, a necessary consequence of public ownership. But privately owned forests also pose issues of public policy because private forestry has always had a substantial public input of one kind or another. Privately owned forests also pose issues of private policy for their owners.

Many kinds of policy issues arise for such forests: how much land to use for forests; how to manage old growth forests during their conversion to regular rotations; how much forest to reserve from cutting for wilderness, environmental, or other reasons; how much to invest and to expend in production of those forest outputs that produce no cash income; how to protect environmental values on forest land; and what policy to follow with respect to exports of forest commodities. These and numerous other issues have arisen in the past and are likely to reappear in the future.

Policy issues are nearly always complex. If they were simple, they would be resolved easily and quickly. A policy issue always involves several contending parties or forces, since there would be no issue over policy if there were only one viewpoint. It is generally difficult to reach an agreement on any issue that satisfies everyone equally. The position of some people is often made worse by a particular policy decision, and some people usually gain more than others. Sometimes, policies are arrived at by sheer political or economic force and sometimes in ways that seem dubiously rational.

Nevertheless, and in spite of the limitations of the policy-making process, a rational and comprehensive framework for analysing policy issues is highly desirable. If unanimous agreement on policy is not possible, the contestants may at least be able to agree on what the disagreement is all about. Arriving at a wise policy decision that will stand the test of time is facilitated by agreement on "facts." But this is far from easy to attain. There may be disagreement on what kinds of information or opinion are relevant facts. One old definition describes a "fact" as: "an opinion not now in dispute." On this basis, the existence of the dispute throws the fact into challenge. The problem is exacerbated because the relevant facts are those related to the future, which is in considerable measure unknown and unknowable.

In the analysis of all natural resource policy issues, I think it necessary to consider five different kinds of facts and to make five different kinds of analyses: (1) physical and biological feasibility and consequences; (2) economic efficiency; (3) economic equity, or who gains and who pays; (4) cultural acceptability; and (5) administrative or operational practicality.

Every use of natural resources has some physical or biological aspects. Some uses of a particular resource are technically easy, others are difficult but possible, and still others are impossible or nearly so. These statements are true for forests as for many other kinds of natural resource situations. Some species of trees may be easily grown in a particular location, others can be grown only poorly or with considerable risk of failure, and still others cannot be grown at all. Soils, climate in all its manifold respects, elevation, position on Earth's surface, and many other factors affect forest growth. Here in the Pacific Northwest we are surrounded by Douglas fir, hemlock, pines, and associated species; we do not encounter natural stands of oak, cypress, hickory, maple, beech, and birch and would find it difficult to grow them here.

In addition to considerations of physical and biological feasibility, there are physical and biological consequences of every resource management action. Whether a forest is cut partially by selective cutting, totally by clearcutting, or to an intermediate degree by another method, the ecosystem will be modified to some extent. Removal of the best trees of some desired species may greatly change the future forest, for instance. This has happened on millions of acres of mixed hardwoods in the South and East, which have been severely degraded by this type of selective removal. If one removes some or all of the trees, in situations where forest regeneration is slow and uncertain, severe physical and biological consequences will follow. It is often less well understood that doing nothing will have physical and biological consequences too. The mature forest, which seems so timeless, permanent, and indestructible to the casual observer, is in fact constantly changing, and some day those old trees will all be blown down, or die and fall, or be killed by fire, disease, or insects.

Just as physical and biological feasibility limit what can be done in resource management, so economic efficiency determines what can be done profitably. Many resource actions are technically feasible but economically impractical. Trees can be planted on poor sites but the costs will exceed the values of the resultant growth. Or old growth trees can be harvested from remote sites, possibly by balloon or helicopter methods, but at costs that far exceed the values. A cutover forested area could be nursed back to a reasonable facsimile of a wilderness in a hundred years or so by careful management and exclusion of nonconforming uses, but would the cost be worth it?

Economic efficiency is typically measured by benefit/cost ratios. More properly, it is the absolute margin of benefit in excess of cost which should be maximized, rather than the ratio between them. Since costs are incurred and benefits are received on different time patterns, it is necessary to compare them on a present value basis by a process of discounting. The choice of interest rate may affect economic feasibility as much as any other single factor that enters into the benefit/cost calculation.

Although benefit/cost calculations are unavoidably only approximate, in part because they deal with an unknown future, and although the benefit/cost analysis has frequently been prostituted by those who distort it to produce their predetermined "answers," a calculation of probable benefits and probable costs is the most powerful tool yet devised for economically sound resource management. The technique is fully usable for forest outputs not marketed for cash. For instance, the forest wildlife specialist with a limited budget must decide where to spend it and for what purposes, and he makes a benefit/cost analysis—even when he protests that he does not.

But economic equity is as important as economic efficiency. Every natural resource management action and every resource policy produce some gains and involve some costs. Frequently, the persons or the groups who secure the gains do not bear the costs, or at least do not bear all of them. Sometimes society as a whole (or general government) bears part of the cost, as for research, fire prevention, roads, and other aspects of forest management. But, of course, government is merely the totality of its citizens, and governmental revenues are simply taxes paid by individuals. Profitable forest management is enormously more difficult because of its "freeloaders," the people who enjoy forest outputs such as water, wildlife, recreation, and wilderness without paying much or anything for them. At the same time, forest owners sometimes impose costs upon other persons— when the quality of water flowing off their land is degraded, for example.

There is no neat test to determine optimum economic

equity, analogous to the benefit/cost criterion for economic efficiency. In the American society we reject complete equality of income as both unattainable and undesirable; we are unwilling to reduce everyone to the same level. We talk about reducing great disparities in income, but have achieved relatively little toward this end. From time to time we are outraged because some individual or some small group reaps a large and undeserved income at public expense. In forestry, we argue that users of wood from public and private forests should pay for the wood they get at as near a fair price as we can estimate. But users of other forest outputs rarely pay for what they receive, and only slowly do we, as a nation, seem to be moving to a policy of making forest users pay for what they get.

Cultural acceptability is my fourth criterion of forest policy. It is not enough that we know how to do something, that it is economically efficient, and that the gains and costs are fairly distributed. The result of our policy must be one that we, as a people, want or at least will accept. For instance, the outcry over some timber harvests arose from dissatisfaction with the appearance of the harvested area. Outrage at slash and defective wood left on the side, at rectangular and unattractive lines bounding harvested areas, and at raw exposed soil was primarily a sociological or cultural phenomenon. If beauty is in the eye of the beholder, so is ugliness. Considerations of biological, economic, and environmental efficiency were dwarfed by rejection of unaesthetic results. Public and private forestry will be more influenced by human attitudes in the future than they have been in the past.

Finally, every resource policy must be capable of being

carried out in practice; otherwise it is useless or worse. Nothing is gained and a good deal may be lost by adopting a policy that cannot be, or is unlikely to be, put into effective operation. If policy requires information that does not exist, or calls for a level of competence in personnel that is unavailable, or for some other reason cannot be or will not be put into operation, it is unproductive of good results and may discredit ideas or organizations that under other conditions might be effective. There is no use urging a small private forest owner to undertake a management program that in fact he cannot carry out, for instance. I have always felt that any attempt at public regulation of private forestry practices would founder on administrative detail, even if it were strongly supported, which I doubt it would be.

The formation of natural resource policy for forests or for any other resource requires a consideration of these five kinds of information and of these five approaches—physical and biological feasibility and consequences, economic efficiency, economic equity, cultural acceptability, and operational or administrative practicality. This is extremely difficult. Because five different kinds of factors are involved, the simple comparison of one with another is impossible. It is impossible to simultaneously maximize each of the five variables, were some complex formula for policy decisions possible.

Because it is so difficult to use five different kinds of data and five different methods of analysis, some persons have argued that a simpler approach must be found. One could, of course, maximize economic efficiency by disregarding economic equity and cultural acceptability. The result would appear neat and decisive but would probably be rejected if an effort were made to apply the proposed policy. Life is complex, not simple; models can abstract part of reality and thereby throw some light on a problem, but their apparent "answer" is nearly always unacceptable or unusable in practice. The problem lies not in the complexity of any method of analysis but in the inherent complexity of natural resource situations in general.

The solution to the complexities of resource policy formation must lie in pragmatic compromises among viewpoints and among forms of analysis. Trade-offs between economic efficiency and economic equity, for example, may not be simple, yet some compromise should be possible. Likewise, trade-offs between other pairs of considerations are necessary. A viable policy rarely involves complete dominance of one viewpoint and complete subservience of all others. An explicit consideration of all relevant factors, with the best pragmatic compromise among divergent approaches, is more likely to produce a good or at least a tolerable solution to complex policy issues than will any superficially simpler but deficient approach.

National Forests, Now and For the Future*

THE national forests are a great national and regional asset but their contribution to the well-being of the American people is substantially less than it could be.

The conservation, environmental, and silvicultural aspects of national forests have been discussed and written about extensively. The conomic or financial aspects have had far less attention. This is strange since the national forests are big business in the American sense of the term. If they were an industrial corporation their gross income for each of the past twenty years or more would have ranked them half way up *Fortune*'s list of the 500 largest industrial business firms, and the value of their assets would have put them higher still. The national forests have important values that are not reflected in their cash revenues, of course. But as public business enterprises they should be subjected to much of the same conomic analysis as are equally large private businesses.

*Some of the tables and charts included herein appeared in my article entitled "The National Forests: A Great National Asset is Poorly Managed and Unproductive" *Science* 191 (20 February 1976): 762–67. Copyright 1976 by the American Association for the Advancement of Science. Permission from *Science* to use these tables and charts is gratefully acknowledged.

The national forests include 187 million acres, or 8 percent of the national land area. Half their area is classified by the Forest Service as "commercial forest"; the other half is unforested, too thinly forested, or too low in wood-growing potential to be considered commercial. My own estimate is that only about a third of the total national forest area has sufficient capacity to justify continued timber management. But even this estimate means 65 million acres nationally or an area approximately the size of Oregon.

The western national forests are dominantly land reserved from the former public domain; the southern and eastern forests were purchased from private landowners. All are managed under the Multiple Use-Sustained Yield Act of 1960, and all are subject to the Forest and Rangeland Renewable Resources Planning Act of 1974. The Forest Service has always emphasized the multiple use aspect of national forests. This requires consideration of timber, recreation, wilderness, watershed, wildlife, and other values and outputs, and my analysis here deals with all of these.

Although the national forests include only 18 percent of the commercial forest land of the nation, they include half the volume of standing softwood timber of sawlog size (but a lesser proportion of hardwood timber). National forests are more heavily stocked than lands of any other major ownership class. Extensive areas in the national forest consist of mature, old-growth timber where net annual growth is low and where rot, disease, and insects take a heavy annual toll. Annual net growth per acre on national forests is lower both in absolute volume and in relation to potential capacity than is the case for any other major ownership category.

OUTPUT OF NATIONAL FORESTS

Output of the national forest system as a whole has increased markedly in the past forty-five years (see table 1). The annual volume of timber harvested has risen more than eight times, annual numbers of recreation visits has increased by thirty times, and the annual output of other national forest services has risen by smaller relative amounts. In particular times and places, one kind of output has been competitive with other kinds of outputs and trade-offs became necessary. But for the system as a whole and for the time period as a whole, it has been possible to produce more of everything.

In spite of this encouraging upward trend in output

Table 1
THE GROWTH IN AVERAGE ANNUAL HARVEST OF OUTPUTS
FROM NATIONAL FORESTS, 1925–29 AND 1968–72

Item	Annual Average 1925–29	1968–72	1968–72 as multiple of 1925–29
Timber cut	1.35[a]	11.54[b]	8.6
Recreation visits	6.3[c]	188[d]	30
Wildlife	216[e]	582[f]	2.7
Water[g]	N.A.	N.A.	probably >2.0

[a] Billion board feet; see *The Federal Lands Since 1956* (Resources for the Future, Washington, 1967), p. 59.

[b] Billion board feet; see *Agricultural Statistics 1974* (USGPO, Washington, 1974), p. 550.

[c] Million recreation visits; see *The Federal Lands Since 1956*, p. 60.

[d] Million visitor days 1973, see *Agricultural Statistics 1974*, p. 554.

[e] Thousand big game killed by hunters, 1940–44 average, see *The Federal Lands Since 1956*, p. 60.

[f] Thousand big game killed by hunters, see *Agricultural Statistics 1974*, p. 555.

[g] No data are available on the use of water flowing off national forests. With the volume of dam building, public and private, *use* in the latter period can hardly be less than double the former, even if total stream flow is unchanged.

of all kinds of services from the national forest system as a whole, present net growth of wood is disappointingly low, both nationally and regionally (see table 2). The gross growth per acre is somewhat less on national forests than on forest-industry forests, reflecting in part the inherently lower productivity of the national forests (about which, more later). The most significant fact is the nearly double mortality loss per acre on national forests as on forest-industry forests. In 1970, net growth on national forests was only 39 percent of potential capacity, whereas on forest industry forests it was 59 percent of capacity. A further unsatisfactory aspect of this situation is that in the past twenty-five years in the coastal Pacific Northwest there has been almost no increase in net timber growth per acre on national forests while net growth was increasingly steadily on every other major class of forest ownership (see table 3).

The poor showing of national forests in timber growing is largely, but not wholly, a corollary of their extensive volumes of old growth mature timber on which net growth per acre is very low. The only way in which more timber can be grown on many national forest areas is to

Table 2
GROSS AND NET GROWTH OF SAWTIMBER PER ACRE OF COMMERCIAL
FOREST IN NATIONAL FORESTS AND FOREST INDUSTRY FORESTS
(United States and Coastal Pacific Northwest, 1970)

Item	U.S. Average		Coastal Pacific Northwest	
	National forests	Forest-industry forests	National forests	Forest-industry forests
Gross growth	176	220	394	468
Mortality loss	68	35	231	128
Net growth	107	185	163	340

NOTE: All statistics are given in board feet.

Table 3
ANNUAL NET GROWTH PER ACRE OF SOFTWOOD GROWING STOCK, BY
OWNERSHIP CLASS
(Pacific Northwest, 1952, 1962, and 1970)

Ownership class	1952	1962	1970
National forests	26	27	27
Other public forests	44	66	78
Forest-industry forests	49	54	61
Other private forests	42	53	64

NOTE: All statistics are given in cubic feet.

cut the timber now standing. There seems a good deal of confusion about the relation between growing and harvesting of timber. Many people realize that cutting cannot long proceed in excess of net growth, because this depletes standing inventory, ultimately to the point of exhaustion. But fewer people seem to realize that growth of timber cannot proceed indefinitely unless timber harvest also goes forward, since inventory cannot accumulate beyond some maximum volume per acre. Growth is essential for harvest, but harvest is essential for net growth. The trees that grow in a forest may be harvested for man's use, or they may be allowed to stand until they die, after which their wood is ultimately consumed by bacteria.

POTENTIAL OF NATIONAL FORESTS

Various land forms or situations within forests can be classified according to their inherent capacity to produce desired forest outputs. This has been done for wilderness to a limited extent; some forested areas are classified as "suitable," and others as "unsuitable" for wilderness. The same can also be done for recreation, wildlife, or other outputs, but such classifications have rarely been made for these outputs. The most common

classification of forest sites is according to their capacity
to grow wood annually. Five site classes have been established in Forest Service data on commercial forests of all
ownership classes. These range from Site Class I, which
can produce 165 or more cubic feet of wood annually, to
Site Class V, which can produce only 20 to 50 cubic feet
of wood annually. Less productive sites are considered
noncommercial. The classification applies to fully
stocked natural stands for the lifetime of the stand. No
consideration is given to the possibility of increasing
wood growth by intensive forest management.

This classification of timber-growing potential is a
biological, not an economic, classification. Each cubic
foot of wood is implicitly considered as valuable as every
other cubic foot of wood. There is no allowance for dif-
ferences in cost of harvesting, including cost of road
building. In other ways, the classification is deficient as a
criterion of economic capacity to grow wood. Nevertheless, the classification does have substantial value, and, in
any event, it is all we have.

The data on forest productive capacity under this
classification system are highly detailed but may be
briefly summarized:

1. The least productive forests occupy a substantial
area but contribute a minor part of the productive potential. Specifically, 27 percent of all commercial forest
area in the United States falls in Site Class V, but only 12
percent of the *productive capacity* falls in this class.

2. Every major forest ownership class includes forests
of a wide range in productivity. The variation in
productivity *within* forest ownership categories is more
impressive than the average difference *between* ownership categories.

3. Because the process of public land disposal in the United States was a selective one, forests owned by forest industries have somewhat more land in the highest productive classes and somewhat less land in the least productive classes than do forests of other ownerships; and the national forests, while less productive in total than forest-industry forests, are about average for all other major ownership classes.

4. When forests of lower productivity are omitted, the average productivity on the various ownership classes is more nearly equal (see table 4). Both the absolute and the relative difference between national forests and forest-industry forests is substantially narrowed by omission of the less productive sites. If timber growing were confined to the more productive sites on national forests, it could be nearly as economic there as on forest-industry forests.

Table 4

U.S. AND COASTAL PACIFIC NORTHWEST AVERAGE CAPACITY FOR ANNUAL WOOD GROWTH

Forest ownership category	U.S. Averages		Coastal Pacific Northwest	
	Including all commercial forest land	Including only forests in Site Classes I to IV	Including all commercial forest land	Including only forests in Site Classes I to III
National forests	76	93	114	141
Other public forests	72	92	138	152
Forest industry forests	88	98	145	160
Other private forests	74	88	128	148
All forests	78	91	131	151

NOTE: All statistics are given in cubic feet of wood per acre annually.

A consideration of potential future productive capacity of national forests requires some definition of "potential." It might be a biological or physical potential to grow wood, provide wilderness, supply outdoor recreation, and so on for other outputs, or it might be an economic potential that took account of values of outputs and costs of producing them. Another factor is the degree to which the national forests are managed for single outputs such as wood, wilderness, or recreation, with output of other products or services strictly subordinate to the dominant one, as contrasted to management for all outputs considered simultaneously. This may be described as the difference between "dominant use" and "multiple use," though I personally find those terms so vague as to be nearly meaningless.

If the national forests were managed to produce the biological potential of each kind of use, their output could be substantially above the present (see table 5). The area biologically suitable for wilderness, for example, is estimated at 55 million acres, if present definitions of wilderness are maintained. The biological potential of wood-growing is very great if intensive forestry is practiced on every acre and if all other outputs are subordinate to wood production. The biological potential is also great for all the other forest outputs. In each case, management for the dominant purpose would still leave much of the output from the subordinate uses. For instance, even if maximum wood growth on every acre of commercial forest were sought, there would still be some nonforested or less heavily forested wilderness areas.

When biological potential is reduced to an economic potential and when consideration is given to other outputs, the potential for each output is still above the

Table 5
PRESENT AND POTENTIAL OUTPUTS OF NATIONAL FORESTS

KIND OF OUTPUT	UNIT	PRESENT OUTPUT[a]	POTENTIAL OUTPUT[b]	
			Biological basis, each use considered dominant and other uses subordinate; no concern for economic efficiency	Reasonably economic basis, and each use adjusted to other uses.
Wood grown annually	Bil. cu. ft.	2.6	10.5	6 to 7
Wilderness area[c]	Mil. acres	11.6	55	40
Outdoor recreation	Mil. visitor days	188	1,000	400
Water yield (volume)		unmeasured	25% more	10% more
Wildlife, all kinds		unmeasured	many more	slightly more

[a]1970 for wood, some more recent year or average of years for others.

[b]Estimates of the author, see text for basis.

[c]Formally designated wilderness areas, excluding "de facto" wilderness. Assumes no major future further relaxation in standards of wilderness, as to size of tracts or degree of nonwilderness use tolerated. Acreage measures, at best, opportunity for wilderness experience, not actual usage.

present. The future economic potential outputs for each good and service exceeds the present output, just as the latter exceeds the outputs of forty-five years ago. Given today's technology, the national forests have a huge unrealized potential. The next fifty years will not see as high relative increases as the past fifty years, but in absolute terms the potentials are greater than the past increases.

Some conflicts among outputs will surely arise, and some trade-offs will be necessary, but the dominant fact is the possibility of more of everything if the national forests are properly managed. There can be both more wilderness and more timber harvest, for instance. The threat to wood production posed by the preservationists lies not in their desire for more wilderness but in their apparent determination to prescribe silvicultural practices on lands used for timber growing.

The key to more of eveything lies in intensive forestry for wood production on the lands most productive for this purpose. Such intensive forestry provides the wood the nation needs and is willing to pay for. Properly managed, it does not impinge adversely on those forest outputs compatible with wood harvest. Most important, it frees some of the more productive forests and all of the less productive ones for other uses, including wilderness.

A FINANCIAL BALANCE SHEET FOR NATIONAL FORESTS

The national forest system may be considered as one large business enterprise, and a financial balance sheet may be prepared (see table 6). A difficult but extremely important aspect is the capital structure. Based on timber, land, and other values determined in private markets, and suitably discounted because of time required to realize such values, the present value of the national forest system is estimated at $42 billion, or $224 per acre of the whole system. Although it is inconceivable that the national forests will ever be sold to private parties, such values would be supported in the private market, and there is no reason why the public enterprise should be managed to produce a lesser social product.

The value is admittedly an estimate, but most of the analysis that follows is unchanged if the value is only half the estimate.

The national forests produce large cash receipts. In addition, substantial road building and other improvements are paid for by timber sold, an "in kind" receipt. Still further, many valuable services are provided free or at nominal prices. Including them at their estimated full value leads to an additional value of services approximately equal to the cash receipts. On the expenditure side there are cash outlays, "in kind" allowances for the roads and other improvements, cash payments to states and counties, and, above all, an interest allowance on the capital tied up in the national forests.

The balance sheet in Table 6 is a bare-bones one, and unfortunately an approximate one since official figures are not published for many of the items. The table, taken alone, does not answer the question: Are the national forests managed economically wisely? The table does include *all* outputs of national forests, not merely those sold for cash, and it includes *all* items of cost, not merely those paid in cash; to this extent it provides the right range of considerations. On this basis, the national forests incurred a huge deficit, equal to about nine dollars per person in the whole population. Another way of putting it is to say that the national forest system earned only 0.5 percent interest on its value, even when full allowance is made for the value of all noncash outputs.

The critical consideration is whether some other management program would have done better. The 1974 Resources Planning Act requires the Forest Service to develop and to defend management plans that will maximize net returns (when all values are taken into

Table 6
FINANCIAL STATEMENT FOR NATIONAL FORESTS, CIRCA 1974.

Account item	Total national forest system (mil. $)	Per acre of		
			Commercial forest acreage	
		Entire acreage ($)	Classes I–V ($)	Classes I–IV ($)
Capital structure:				
Value of standing timber[a]	20,000	107	217	324
Value of forest land[b]	20,000	107	217	324
Undepreciated value of manmade improvements[c]	2,000	11	22	32
Total assets	42,000	224	456	680
Cash investment[d]	196	1.05	2.13	3.08
Investment in kind[e]	120	.64	1.30	1.94
Value of increased timber inventory, 1970 volume, 1974 prices[f]	42	.22	.46	.68
Income:				
In cash[g]	486	2.60	5.28	7.88
In kind[h]	220	1.18	2.39	3.56
Additional value of products and services provided at less than full market prices[i]	490	2.62	5.32	7.93
total annual output[j]	1,238	6.63	13.45	20.05
Expenditures:				
In cash, all purposes	488	2.62	5.31	7.91
In kind[k]	220	1.18	2.39	3.56
Depreciation of manmade assets, 10%	200	1.07	2.17	3.24
Payment to States and Counties	79	.42	.86	1.28
Interest on all assets, 5%	2,100	11.23	22.80	34.00
Total	3,087	16.51	33.53	49.99
Net annual income, cash & noncash	(1,849)	(9.87)	(20.08)	(29.94)

[a] *The Outlook for Timber in the United States* shows a 1970 inventory of 1,021 billion board feet of sawtimber on national forests. On the basis of $40 per 1,000 board feet, which is an approximate recent average for timber sold from national forests, the value of the standing sawtimber (ignoring values for growing stock of less than sawtimber size)

would be slightly in excess of $40 billion. This value has been cut in half, to reflect a reasonably early (10 to 20 year) liquidation value.

[b] Excludes timber values; averages $107 per acre for all national forest land; also assumes reasonably early liquidation value.

[c] *The Federal Lands Since 1956*, p. 54, report $1,160 million in 1963; estimated to have risen to $2,000 million by 1974.

[d] Data from Forest Service (personal letter 17 July 1975 from John R. McGuire, with enclosures); roads, trails, other construction, and purchase of land.

[e] Road building allowance in timber sales contracts; 12 billion board feet, assumed $10 per 1,000 board feet road building allowance in sale price.

[f] *The Outlook for Timber in the United States* shows that in 1970 harvest slightly exceeded growth of growing stock for softwoods but that growth exceeded harvest by about 450 million cubic feet for hardwood growing stock. Converted to board feet, 6 board feet per cubic foot; $80 per 1,000 board feet for softwood, $30 per 1,000 for hardwood.

[g] Includes receipts from mineral leases on national forest lands acquired by purchase from private owners; excludes them from national forest lands reserved from public domain.

[h] All of road building allowance plus $100 million in working funds, cooperative agreements, etc. where the national forest user agrees or is required as a condition of timber harvest or other use to undertake certain restoration or other activities.

[i] Estimated on basis of 170 million recreation visits other than wilderness at an average value of $2 each, 10 million wilderness area visits at an average value of $10 each, and water supply at $50 million. Wildlife values assumed included in recreation and wilderness values. States may benefit from wildlife values, for instance in sale of hunting licenses. No allowance is made for the possibility wood and forage are sold at less than a full value.

[j] Increased timber inventory, cash and kind receipts, and values of products not sold for cash.

[k] These are the same items described in [h]; they appear both as income and as outlay.

account). Economic rationality will require a matching of marginal costs of management with marginal values (all services fully valued).

EXPENDITURES AND INCOME BY REGIONS, FORESTS, AND SITES

For the five most recent years for which data are available, the regional pattern of expenditures for national forest operation and for investment was economically wasteful (see figures 1 and 2). Nearly as much money was spent in each region where receipts were small as in each region where receipts were large. The Pacific Northwest was particularly short-changed in both operating and investment outlays. These charts use only cash receipts and cash expenditures because only these data are published by regions. Inclusion of noncash incomes would raise the level of total income, while inclusion of noncash costs (especially interest) would raise the level of expenditures. But it is by no means clear that the relation between expenses and income would be changed thereby.

The relation between total cash expenditures and total cash income on each of the national forests is equally uneconomic (see figure 3). While there is considerable variation among forests in both cash expenditures and in cash revenues, little more is spent on national forests with large revenues than on national forests with very low revenues. Again, data on all income, including noncash values, and on all expenditures, including noncash costs, would raise the level of income and of expenditures, respectively, without necessarily affecting the relation between them.

Other data, too detailed to present here, show that timber management costs per 1000 board feet are higher in regions where timber values are lower, and that average expenditures per national forest are as high in regions where the national forest lands are relatively unproductive as they are in regions of the highest productivity. Still other analyses show that the national forest system as a whole has an excessive amount of capital tied up in mature slow-growing forests. My esti-

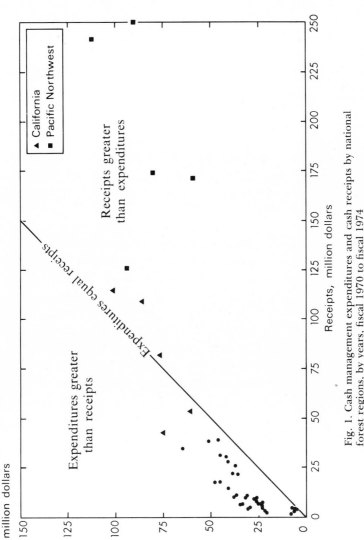

Fig. 1. Cash management expenditures and cash receipts by national forest regions, by years, fiscal 1970 to fiscal 1974

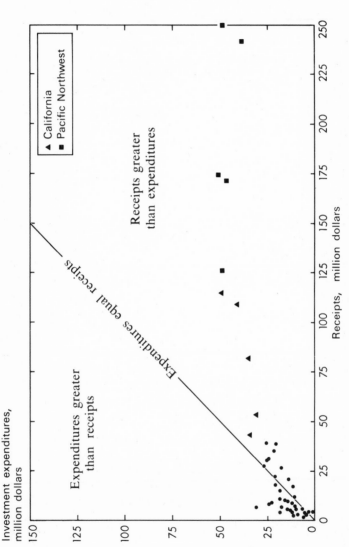

Fig. 2. Cash investment expenditures and cash receipts by national forest regions, by years, fiscal 1970 to fiscal 1974

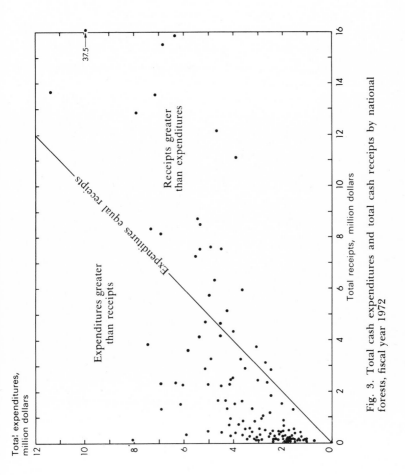

Fig. 3. Total cash expenditures and total cash receipts by national forests, fiscal year 1972

mate is that the annual interest cost of excessive forest inventory is $600 million, or $3 per capita of the whole population.

From the foregoing information and on the basis of such additional information as does exist, it seems highly probable that national forest expenditures are unwisely distributed among sites of different productivity classes. Too much money is spent in timber management on low productivity sites and not enough is spent on sites of high productivity.

While the data are better for wood production than for other forest outputs, and hence the analysis can be more specific for this output, the relationships I have outlined for wood apply generally to all forest outputs.

One can only conclude that the national forests have been managed with virtually no regard for costs and returns. Funds have been spent on economically unrewarding places, kinds of land, and activities; as a result, the national forests are not producing as much of any kind of output as they economically could, while at the same time costs are higher than necessary. A more serious consideration is that they will continue to be relatively unproductive unless major changes are made in their management.

ELEMENTS OF ECONOMIC MANAGEMENT OF NATIONAL FORESTS

In its simplest terms, an economically rational management of the national forests would require a balancing of all costs and all values for each kind of activity for every site or location within the national forest system. Values would include estimates for wilderness, wildlife, water, recreation, and other outputs normally not sold for cash or sold for nominal prices. Costs would include payments "in kind" as well as cash costs and also a capital charge equal to interest from alternative investment of the same funds. The relevant comparison would be marginal costs and marginal values, not average costs and average values.

If managed in this way, national forests would make their greatest contribution to the national well-being. In general, their output would be well above present levels. Their costs per unit of output would surely be less than at present.

There would, of course, be many and difficult problems in applying these basic rules to the management of the national forests. Care would have to be exercised that the processes implicit in these standards did not become too costly and involved. Elaborate benefit/cost analyses are not necessary for every situation; informed and sound judgment may often be adequate if the standards and criteria are kept clearly in mind. Reasonable approximations may be as useful as precise determinations. Present divergences from these principles are so large that major improvement should be possible on the basis of accurate but not highly refined estimates.

ACHIEVEMENT OF NATIONAL FOREST POTENTIALS

If the economic potential of the national forests is to be achieved, policies and operating procedures must be changed in at least three ways:

1. An alert, intelligent, concerned, and continuous national leadership is basic. This includes presidential, Office of Management and Budget, secretarial, and congressional leadership, as well as Forest Service leadership. The potential of the national forests must be

recognized. Adequate plans must be developed, and new methods of operation on the ground actually carried out. The Forest and Rangeland Renewable Resources Planning Act of 1974 offers a substantial opportunity for improvement, but the interest and competence of persons in major administrative positions is critical.

2. New procedures and new analyses of national forest operations are necessary. More searching analysis is needed to ensure that all benefits (at the margin) exceed all costs (at the margin), including noncash as well as cash benefits and costs, for every activity in every location. Funds must be provided to implement plans arrived at in this way. The appropriation process might directly relate all costs to all values, a public corporation to manage the national forests might be established, or the general objectives might be achieved in some other way.

3. In addition to the two preceding changes, which primarily involve governmental units other than the Forest Service, a massive infusion of new blood into the Forest Service is essential. Realization of the productive potential of the national forests will require truly major changes in the philosophy, mental attitudes, and operating techniques of the Forest Service. Its massive organizational inertia, its moderate rate of personnel turnover, and the likelihood that normal replacement would lead to only slow evolution make a major and rapid change in personnel essential. New kinds of professional personnel are needed at all levels and in sufficient numbers to significantly modify the organization.

If management were redirected as outlined here, the

national forests would still not produce large profits for the people of the United States, but their economic record would be vastly better than it now is. The real payoff for the American people would be a larger volume of all forest goods and services—more wilderness, more recreation, and more wood.

Selected References

This is a short list of relatively recent, relatively accessible books and reports, each authoritative but not highly technical. They in turn provide additional sources, to the person interested to follow any specific subject more deeply.

Bosselman, Fred and David Callies. *The Quiet Revolution in Land Use Control*. Council on Environmental Quality, December 1971.

Clawson, Marion, *America's Land and Its Uses*. Baltimore: The Johns Hopkins University Press, for Resources for the Future, 1972.

——— *Forests for Whom and for What?* Baltimore: The Johns Hopkins University Press, for Resources for the Future, 1975.

——— *The Economics of National Forest Management*. Baltimore: The Johns Hopkins University Press, for Resources for the Future, Working Paper EN-6, 1976.

Downs, Anthony, *Opening Up the Suburbs: An Urban Strategy for America*. New Haven: Yale University Press, 1973.

Gregory, G. R. *Forest Resource Economics*. New York: Ronald Press, 1972.

Healy, Robert G. *Land Use and the States*. Baltimore: The Johns Hopkins University Press, for Resources for the Future, 1976.

Kaufman, Herbert. *The Forest Ranger*. Baltimore: The Johns Hopkins University Press, 1967.

McAllister, Donald M., ed. *Environment: A New Focus for Land-use Planning*. Washington, D.C.: National Science Foundation, October 1973.

Perloff, Harvey S., ed. *Agenda for the New Urban Era*. Chicago: American Society of Planning Officials, 1975.

Reilly, William K., ed. *The Use of Land: A Citizens Policy Guide to Urban Growth*. New York: Thomas Y. Crowell Company, 1973.

Spurr, Stephen and Burton Barnes. *Forest Ecology*. New York: Wiley, 1962.

Worrell, Albert. *Principles of Forest Policy*. New York: McGraw-Hill, 1970.

MARION CLAWSON, *currently a consultant to Resources for the Future, Inc., began his distinguished career in the field of land use and resource management with a course in general agriculture taken at the University of Nevada. He later was awarded the doctor of philosophy degree in economics from Harvard University and spent the following twenty-four years in the service of the United States government. While working in the Bureau of Agricultural Economics of the Department of Agriculture, he directed extensive studies of agricultural development on major irrigation projects. From 1948 to 1953 he was director of the Bureau of Land Management of the Department of the Interior. He spent the following two years as an economic consultant in Israel and has since completed shorter, similar assignments in Pakistan, Venezuela, Chile, and India.*

From 1955 to 1973, Dr. Clawson was director of the Land and Water Program of Resources for the Future, Inc., a nonprofit private research and educational institution financed by the Ford Foundation. During 1974–75 he was acting president of Resources for the Future and in 1976 became a consultant to that organization.

Dr. Clawson was once president of the Western Agricultural Economics Association, vice-president of the American Economics Association, and executive secretary and later vice-president of the Society for International Development. He also was a member of the Committee on Renewable Resources for Industrial Materials of the National Academy of Sciences. He has been a member and officer of various other professional organizations as well. He is currently a fellow of the American Agricultural Economics Association. From the autumn of 1971 to the autumn of 1973 he served as a member of the President's Advisory Panel on Timber and the Environment.

In addition to his many other achievements, Dr. Clawson has written exten-

sively in the area of land use and resource management. Among his publications are Forests for Whom and for What? *(1975)*, Suburban Land Conversion in the United States *(1971)*, Policy Directions for U.S. Agriculture *(1968), and* The Federal Lands since 1956 *(1967). The volumes he has edited include* Forest Policy for the Future *(1975) and* Modernizing Urban Land Policy *(1973).*